Cornwall
SHIPWRECKS

North Coast

The wooden diving barrel used by John Lethbridge in 1725-40 to recover treasure and cargo from shipwrecks in Cornwall. RICHARD LARN COLLECTION

For further information of all the titles in this series please visit:-
www.tormark.co.uk

First published 2009 by Tor Mark, United Downs Ind Est, Redruth,
Cornwall TR16 5HY

ISBN 978 085025 415 0

© 2009 Tor Mark

Acknowledgements

Front cover: mv RMS *Mulheim* wrecked at Gamper Bay (Apex Photo Agency)

This page: The Austrian barque *Capricorno* slipped her tug off Lundy. A gale
drove her onto the breakwater at Bude – 27 December 1900
(Richard Larn Collection)

Inside back cover: mv RMS *Mulheim* (Apex Photo Agency)

Back cover: www.aqua-photography.com – photo by K J Hunkin

All other pictures acknowledged under image

Printed by R Booth Ltd, The Praze, Penryn, Cornwall TR10 8AA

It comes as no surprise that the North Cornwall coast has claimed in excess of 2000 recorded wrecks. Everything has conspired to make this one of the most treacherous areas in the world. The cliffs and headlands are higher and the offshore reefs sharper, the number of safe refuges fewer than on the south coast. In addition, the north coast suffers the fury of the Atlantic gales.

The safe anchorages are not only fewer than on the south coast, but also much smaller – St Ives, Portreath, Newquay, Port Isaac and Boscastle can only accommodate small vessels of the coastal and fishing industry. Ironically, the one haven of any size that could take larger vessels, Padstow had its own severe restrictions. Over the years the harbour has been plagued by its shallow waters and treacherous sandbanks known as the Doom Bar. Over 350 ships are recorded as being lost in the Padstow area alone, the earliest in 1618 and the last to date in 1997. Until the mid 18th century there was not a single lighthouse or cliff beacon between the Longships, off Land's End and Lundy Island, a distance of approximately 100 miles.

In earlier times, it was Bristol merchants who complained to government of the lack of lights on the north coast of Cornwall, but it was 1795 before anything was done. This resulted in the Longships lighthouse being built, the first in the area, followed by Lundy Island in 1820, Trevose Head in 1847, Hartland Point in 1874 and Pendeen in 1900. With an average interval of 25 years between each new lights construction, just four in one century, Trinity House and HM Government appear to have been dilatory to say the least.

Britain's centuries-old reliance on coal, and its abundance in South Wales, led to the creation of the Welsh coal ports; an equally important factor in the history of north Cornwall was the Cornish copper mining industry. Passing ships in ballast would call in to load copper ore, transport it to Swansea, Cardiff or Newport, and then load with coal for their return passage. This continuous shuffling of ships back and forth led to many of them being wrecked, due to a myriad of causes, ranging from drunken skippers to fog, lack of charts, gales, badly maintained ships, leaks and even deliberate sabotage by crews intent on a short voyage.

This publication deliberately covers a select number of wreck incidents, some of which are both old and obscure, others less so, illustrating the nature of the ships, what they carried and their cause of loss. Today, the search for and exploration of shipwrecks is assuming national importance, with English Heritage offering Wreck Protection and the Nautical Archaeological Society (NAS) running courses and field events that amplify a new national awareness that shipwrecks are important. With literally hundreds of divers eagerly putting to sea at weekends, in the hope of finding either a new wreck or exploring one already known, maritime archaeology and sunken ships have assumed a new and important role, one that our forebears could never have imagined.

RICHARD & BRIDGET LARN
St Mary's, Isles of Scilly 2009

Galleon Rock

c1550 – Porth Quin Bay, near Padstow

Researching in 1971 for shipwreck information concerning Rumps Point and the Mouls, a huge rock outcrop to the NW in Port Quin Bay, near Padstow, Richard Larn and the late Roy Davies visited the home of a Padstow fisherman, then well into his 80s. He lived in a small cottage near Polzeath, and after being invited in by his wife she remarked, 'He's very deaf so you will have to speak up; he's also very forgetful, so don't expect too much'. We told him we were divers looking for shipwrecks in the area. Could he remember any wrecks from the old days? Perhaps stories passed down by his grandfather?

We were talking about the steamship *Sphene* that he had seen go down in 1946 off Port Quin, when suddenly he said, 'There's the Spanish wreck on Galleon Rock. Do you know about that one, boys?' He proceeded to tell us a remarkable story that was almost unbelievable. His grandfather found the site he said, before WW1; they used to lay crab pots around it and shellfish would come up a rusty colour, as they do when there's iron on the seabed. 'It's where a Spanish ship sank a long time ago', he said. 'Grandfather said his father had told him 'twas a Spanish Armada vessel, you know, with guns and all'. Roy and I looked at each other in disbelief. We knew of an Armada vessel wrecked off Bideford, its nine iron cannon still mounted in Victoria Park. There is displayed in the Town Hall a huge iron 'treasure chest' supposedly from the same wreck – but an Armada wreck of 1588 off Padstow – surely not?

'This Galleon Rock you mentioned', Richard asked, 'we have never seen that on a chart, where is it?' 'You won't see it on no chart, boy', he replied, 'it don't show, it's a ledge on a sandy bottom and it's deep; remember the marks if you want them?'

The fisherman's blue eyes twinkled, he was obviously enjoying our discussion, and related the shore marks which Richard wrote down. Two days later the divers were out in Port Quin Bay on a boat, trying to make sense of the marks the old boy had given them. These involved a coastguard lookout, a dip in a rock face on the Mouls, something on Kelland Head, but the echo-sounder showed only a flat featureless seabed at 35m. The divers went back to Polzeath, knocked on the old fisherman's door. He was sitting in his rocking chair as before, 'What can I do for yer?' he asked. We explained that his marks made no sense and we had found nothing of Galleon Rock. He looked first at one of us then the other, 'I don't know what you are talking about, and where's this Galleon Rock?' he said, 'and I have certainly never met you two before'. His wife apologised as she showed us out, 'I'm sorry', she said, 'he gets like this from time to time, it can last a day or sometimes a month, don't be offended'.

Reluctant to accept that it was all fantasy, Richard and Roy went back to Port Quin Bay, dropped four buoys in a huge square and quartered it with an echo sounder. About an hour later, the sounder trace suddenly leapt up, stayed there for a few seconds, then fell back as the boat passed some obstruction in 38m. As they donned their diving gear the atmosphere was electric – was this Galleon Rock? Might this actually be a galleon wreck of the Armada, or simply a seabed outcrop, home to a few sea urchins and starfish? The sight that greeted their eyes was unbelievable. They landed on a rock ledge rising 3m above the surrounding sand, and scattered across it lay four bronze guns! Not huge 3-ton cannon, but 6ft long thin swivel guns, three complete with their mountings. To find one bronze gun in a lifetime is every diver's dream, to find four at once was unbelievable. Using his underwater slate, Richard carefully drew a plot of how the guns lay and took measurements, plus sketches of their mountings, cascabels (part of the mechanism of a breech loading cannon), tiller slots and barrel markings, such as they were. The divers also noted there was iron concretion (hard mineral matter formed around objects caused by the action of mineral salts over a long period of time), some lead shot and the iron barrel of a pistol showing, all positive indications of a very early wreck.

One of the four historic bronze guns found at the site of an unidentified wreck at Galleon Rock. They were muzzle loading canon, fitted with mounting 'spikes', with evidence of iron 'tillers' by which they were aimed. They are thought to be Spanish c 1570-80, and may have come from a small vessel associated with the Armada of 1588.

RICHARD LARN COLLECTION

Helped by Brian Smith, a friend and diver who kept a fishing boat with lifting facilities at Rock, opposite Padstow, the four guns were raised and taken ashore. They required very little cleaning but had suffered some corrosion over 400 years exposed on the seabed. Colin Carpenter of Ivybridge, a leading expert on the subject of historic weapons, identified them as c1570-80. He classified them as 'port pieces' in the Minion class of early brass guns. One was sold to the late Robin Wiggington, who was in the antique weapons business in Stratford; another went on display in Padstow Museum, the other two eventually found their way to the Unites States.

What ship they came from may never be known. Perhaps the vessel had been a lightly armed merchant vessel acting as a stores ship for the Spanish Armada, or of another period engaged in peaceful trading? The archives in Seville have no record of an Armada ship lost off Padstow, or Bideford for that matter, and the Spanish Treasury and Domestic State Papers of this country offer no clues. It was a remarkable find, resulting from that casual meeting in Polzeath. When the divers returned to thank the fisherman and show him photographs of the guns and artefacts some weeks later, he had unfortunately passed away, and regrettably the opportunity was lost.

Thornton

February 1700 – Port Quin Bay, near Padstow

One of the wreck stories passed on by the same fisherman at Polzeath who told the story of Galleon Rock, was a tale about the 'Screamers'. The cliffs under the old castle at Doydon Point in Port Quin Bay are steep and lonely. Close by, the two divers were told, is a cove, which had long been called the 'Screamers' by locals. It was said to have acquired its name from the dreadful sound of human voices screaming for help when a large ship was wrecked there many, many years ago. Unfortunately, the name and the year of the wreck had long been forgotten, so the divers were faced with yet another challenge: to see if anything of the ship remained and if it did, then to identify the wreck – but where would one start such a quest?

Many lists and accounts of Cornish shipwrecks were scoured but were of no help, so the diver's turned to the Calendars of Domestic State Papers, which are collections of general correspondence prior to c1740. These relate to anything from highwaymen to customs & excise, naval battles to smallpox, marriage to shipwrecks, but it was impossible to read even a fraction of the thousands of volumes involved without a date in mind. Then by chance, Richard got lucky. Whilst researching English East India Company ships at the India Office Records in Waterloo Road, London, a list of late 17th century ships built for the company in the East India Yard at Deptford, made reference to the *Thornton*, lost near

Padstow in 1700. This looked promising, even more so when documents in file IOR. Folio.B/41 revealed the name Port Quinn, spelt as two words with a double 'n' in those days. It transpired that having been built in 1696, armed with 34 cannon and prepared for sea, she left for India and the Far East on her maiden voyage that year which was successfully completed. On 5 March 1698, she left the Downs for Madras on her second voyage, still under Captain William Petrie, carrying a crew of 100. She reached Madras safely, conducted her business and was on the return voyage when things went wrong. Off the Isles of Scilly, she met with a fearful easterly gale and heavy seas, which forced her commander to seek shelter under the high cliffs of north Cornwall. Then the wind veered into the west increasing to hurricane force, and the *Thornton* was forced to run before the wind. The Camel estuary and Padstow harbour with its notorious Doom Bar

Artefacts from the Thornton *showing two knife handles, a watch or clock key; an ornamental button and lead musket shot. The circular lead object is unidentified, possibly a pot lid.*

RICHARD LARN COLLECTION

were no haven for a 500-ton deep laden ship, so Captain Petrie sought the shelter of the Rumps, a headland protecting Port Quin Bay. Here she anchored, but when the wind veered into the north, she parted her cables and drove ashore under high cliffs. Unable to launch her boats due to huge seas, it was the voices of her crew and passengers, many of whom were female with young children, that led to the dreadful 'screaming' heard by the locals, who were unable to reach them, and why that name, 'The Screamers', was given to that part of the coast.

Did anything of the wreck remain? Again, Richard and Roy dived Port Quin Bay, this time under the cliffs in shallow water, and there they found timbers, evidence of an old shipwreck. It had obviously been salvaged at sometime in the past, which was hardly surprising. Homeward bound East Indiamen carried valuable spices, cloth, exotic wood, ivory and porcelain from the Far East. Now all that remained were a couple of iron cannon, the broken shank of an anchor and fragments of lead and brass. Two finds in particular are worth a mention, a cluster of coins found by Richard and a badly eroded ship's bell found by the late Frank Perry of St Blazey, who had joined the team.

St Anthony

Christmas Eve 1741 – Ralph's Cupboard, Illogan

The coast of north Cornwall to the west of Portreath is singularly uninviting to any type of ship whether large or small, and of choice vessels stay well offshore between St Agnes Head and Godrevy Island. Here the cliffs bear forbidding names such as Death Valley, Deadman's Cove, and Hell's Mouth, whilst three small islands named the Gull, Samphire and the Crane, lie scattered offshore. A little to the east of Samphire Island lies an insignificant un-named rock strewn cove which at low tide dries out to reveal a pocket handkerchief sized sandy beach, overlooked by 200ft high cliffs.

Neither locals nor holidaymakers visit this place, which is dark and forbidding since it sees little sun, and access is both difficult and dangerous. Yet, for a short time in 1741, it became the focus of attention of literally thousands of Cornish 'wreckers' from Hayle to Redruth, all intent on plunder. The attraction was of course a shipwreck, 'Bounty from the sea' as they called it in those days, and this was no ordinary wreck. It was in fact a hapless Spanish vessel named *St Anthony*, said to be of some 200-tons, on passage from the Canary Islands to London, accidentally blown north into the Bristol Channel by a gale. She went ashore during the night of Christmas Eve 1741, and not one soul survived when she broke up in the shallows. Once the news had spread every able-bodied male for miles around was drawn to the scene. Tin mines were deserted, farms and animals left unattended, labourers dropped their tools, and more than one invalid left his sickbed, all intent on an orgy of plunder and looting.

The cargo carried in the wreck consisted of logwood, indigo, which was a valuable violet-blue dye, and a huge quantity of silver coin and bullion. The first Cornishmen on the beach next morning were soon filling their pockets with silver – Spanish 8 Reales, known as 'pieces-of-eight', the equivalent of an English crown worth five-shillings, found loose in the beach detritus. Amongst the scattered clothing and other belongings of the crew, someone found a leather pocket book, the cover of which bore the name Walter Brown. This assisted the authorities in identifying the wreck, the London Guildhall Library confirming that a Walter Brown had been the English captain of the ship *St Anthony* of Cadiz, chartered in the West Indies to carry a valuable cargo back to London.

Whether or not the deep cavern in the cove close to a stream, which waterfalls down onto the beach was always known as 'Ralph's Cupboard', or acquired the name following the wreck is uncertain. Perhaps it bears reference to a local smuggler named Ralph reputed to have hidden contraband in the cleft, or possibly someone of that name who found treasure from the wreck hidden there. It is known from old custom records that everything was stolen including all the silver, which was taken up by the country fellows in the neighbour-hood who demolished the whole ship in a few hours. When soldiers and the customs officer from St Ives arrived on the scene to take charge, there was precious little left for them to protect, and they departed empty-handed.

In 1978 a number of diving enthusiasts which included the authors, having formed a group named NAS(SW) (Nautical Archaeological Society – South West) made a project of visiting 'Ralph's Cupboard', to search for possible remains of the *St Anthony* wreck. A spring tide period was chosen when the maximum amount of beach would be exposed at mid-day, and a proton magnetometer, several metal detectors, crowbars and shovels were transported to the site in anticipation. The magnetometer, an instrument capable of detecting ferrous material buried deep beneath the surface, soon gave several huge readings. An iron cannon, round shot and a broken anchor were uncovered by digging, but no silver bars or coins were found that day. Whilst the beach area was thoroughly searched using electronics and probes, rods pushed deep into the sand, all too soon, the tide returned and the search was abandoned. However, a second visit proved worthwhile, since whilst digging around a detected metal contact Richard unearthed a fabulous cluster of sixteen silver coins. This proved to be such a remarkable and unique artefact that it remains intact to this day, the temptation to break it open resisted so that the type, denomination and actual date of the coins remains unknown. Due to their size, they are thought to be Pillar Dollars, probably minted in Mexico or Lima.

A cluster of sixteen silver coins found in 'Ralph's Cupboard' by the authors in 1978. They are probably Spanish American pillar dollars, equal to a crown (five shillings).

RICHARD LARN COLLECTION

Boscawen

24 November 1745 – St. Ives

Whilst St Ives was once the home port of a huge fishing fleet and regularly visited by vessels in the coasting trade, its harbour was always very small. Until the late 18th century there was only a tiny medieval pier, its location now well inside the present harbour area, which offered little shelter from northerly gales. The size of the port and the lack of any great depth of water, plus its inability to shelter a large vessel directly brought about the wreck of the 600-ton *Boscawen*.

She had been built as the French 40-gun frigate *Medée* and captured by Lord Boscawen in the English Channel in 1744. Taken into English service having been released by an Admiralty Prize Court as a legitimately captured enemy vessel, she was renamed after her captor, and then became a privateer under Commodore George Walker. Privateers were armed merchant vessels whose captain carried a letter of marque, a document issued by the Admiralty allowing the ship to engage in legal piracy; their task was to stop and examine ships thought to be carrying cargo for the French or its allies. If this proved to be the case, then the ship and contents were seized, and an Admiralty Prize Court would determine its value and disposal, the privateer's crew and sponsors being awarded prize money, often considerable sums.

French frigates, never as sturdy or well built as their English counterparts carried fewer guns, and whilst being converted to a privateer, her complement of cannon was increased to navy standards, but the results proved disastrous. She encountered a severe gale after leaving the Azores in October 1745; she rode the storm heavily, springing numerous leaks, then her main-yard slings parted, the crew having failed to secure it with chains in time. The huge yard weighing several tons dropped fair and square across both gunwales, doing a great deal of damage. With her crew now in a state of near mutiny, even drawing up a petition demanding they head for home, her captain had little option but to agree.

By the time land was sighted on 24 November, the privateer was virtually a floating wreck with over 12 feet of water in her hold, the crew exhausted from working the pumps day and night to keep afloat. It was then realised that the land mass off to starboard was not the Lizard but Land's End, and that the wind prevented them from making for either Falmouth or Plymouth. With her upper deck awash, distress signal flags fluttering in her rigging, her ensign inverted and signal guns booming out a call for assistance, she hove too offshore in St Ives Roads. Unfortunately, she no longer carried any anchors, since these along with most of her guns, had long since been dropped overboard in the Bay of Biscay to lighten the ship. Neither did she carry any boats, these having been washed off the upper deck by heavy seas. She was far too deep in the water to enter the miniscule St Ives harbour, nor could she be run ashore on the beach, so the officers and crew could only watch and pray as the wind drove her on to the rocks outside the harbour where she broke in two. Men from the town waded out into the surf with lines in an attempt to save the crew, whilst others manned rowing boats and went out to the wreck despite heavy seas, regardless of their own safety.

Commodore Walker remained with the ship until the last seaman, who was injured, was lowered out of the great cabin window into a local boat, only then would he allow them to help him reach the shore. It was a remarkable achievement and a tribute to the ship's officers and locals alike, that only four lives were lost that day out of 200 men on board. Abandoned as a total wreck, the Commodore gave the wreck to the town, telling the mayor to make what they could of his ship. The locals collected her store of provisions, made use of her ropes and rigging, fittings and timbers, finally recovering the few remaining cannon, which were sold by the Mayor at a handsome profit for the town.

Built for the Admiralty as the oiler Scotol *in 1916, she was sold to Hemsley Bell Ltd in 1948 who renamed her* Hemsley 1. *She was on passage to Antwerp for breaking when she went ashore in Fox's Cove, west of Treyarnon Bay, in dense fog and a gale on 12 May 1969.*

WESTERN MORNING NEWS

Hanover

6 December 1763 – St Agnes

A Government packet service to carry mail, despatches, bullion, specie (money) and passengers safely between Corunna, Lisbon and Falmouth was established in 1689, initially with three ships ensuring a regular 14-day service between England and Iberia. The outgoing mail and despatches originating from anywhere in Britain, were collected in London then taken under armed escort by coach to Falmouth. Here it was put on board the privately owned packet ships on hire to the Post Office, which were fast, armed vessels operated on similar lines to ships of the Royal Navy. In time the service expanded to Gibraltar, Malta, South America and the West Indies, as British influence continued to expand. Slowly the number of packet ships increased and by 1800 there were 39 employing 1,200 officers and men, plus an army of shore based clerks, store-keepers, agents, lawyers, bankers, clergy, dockers and labourers. They carried over 3,000 passengers a year, and in 1757 transported £1.5 million in gold and silver to Falmouth. It is quite remarkable that only one packet vessel was lost in British waters, which was the *Hanover* in 1763; more surprisingly is the fact it was wrecked not in the vicinity of Falmouth or on the south coast, but to the north, near St Agnes.

The *Hanover* left Falmouth on her last outward voyage on 24 October 1763, spent 14 days in Lisbon, then sailed for Falmouth on 21 November carrying 39 crew and an indeterminate number of wealthy passengers, reported variously to be between 11 and 40. In addition to mail and passengers, she also carried £67,500 in gold moidar coin in a secure iron chest, which today would be worth around £1.82 million. She also carried a heavy and illegal private cargo against all Post Office rules, which almost certainly contributed to her loss, but this only became known after the wreck was located and partially excavated in 1997, 234 years later. After suffering heavy weather in the Bay of Biscay, she ran into a fearful easterly gale in the English Channel, which blew her west beyond Falmouth and the Lizard causing her captain, Commander Joseph Sherburn, to make the fatal decision to round Land's End seeking the shelter of the north coast. Off Pendeen, whilst preparing to anchor, the crew and passengers were horrified when the wind not only veered from east to north-west, but also increased in strength to hurricane force, leaving them close in on a lee shore. The storm proved stronger than anyone in Cornwall could remember and by now the *Hanover* was in very serious trouble. She was close inshore at night with an onshore gale blowing. Under mere scraps of canvas she clawed her way NE past Gurnard's Head, then St Ives and St Agnes, where she was driven inside of the Bawden Rocks, better known today as the 'Man & his Man'. Here she anchored; the crew cut down both masts to reduce the windage, then throwing overboard her cannon to lighten the ship. With the vessel in total distress, the crew probably cursed Commander Sherburn for taking on board that illegal cargo, and in turn Sherburn himself probably regretted his greed.

At some time during the night, she dragged ashore stern first under 300ft high cliffs, NE of St Agnes, breaking up in a rock gully. Only three out of her crew of 39 and an indeterminate number of passengers survived, two seamen and a boy being found stuck part way up the sheer cliffs next morning by passing tin miners on their way to work. The authorities having been informed, armed guards kept watch against wreckers who were already crowding the cliff top, whilst on the beach men probed the wreck with iron rods in hope of finding the iron treasure chest, which was by now buried deep in sand. It was not until 1763, two years later, that the chest became uncovered and was taken up, its contents intact. The body of Commander Sherburn was laid to rest in Falmouth parish church, since in keeping with most packet captains' he had made Little Falmouth his home. Other bodies found amongst the rocks were buried in St Agnes churchyard. The place where the *Hanover* was lost became known locally as Hanover Cove, a name found on maps and charts of the area to this day.

In 1994 local salvage divers, Colin Martin and Gerald Cameron relocated the wreck, claiming to have found the ship's bell bearing the embossed legend *Hanover Pacquet – 1757*. They also found a beautiful gold mourning ring bearing the inscription Mary Sherburn Obit 16 Feb 1748. Age 22 years. Mary Sherburn was the deceased wife of Captain Sherburn, having died in childbirth. What better proof could one ask for regarding the identification of a wreck?

The bronze bell from the Hanover, *its hanging tabernacle was broken in the wreck.*
RICHARD LARN COLLECTION

The beautiful and ornate gold mourning ring of the captain's deceased wife Mary. The gemstone is missing.

By 1997, Martin had raised sufficient money from backers to mount a full scale salvage operation. He used an offshore jack-up platform complete with crane as a diving platform directly over the site, which was unaffected by tide or weather. This was the first time such a rig had been employed for this purpose in Gt Britain. Media attention attracted a lot of investors, who poured money into the operation, hoping that either the gold moidars were still there, or that wealthy passengers had carried

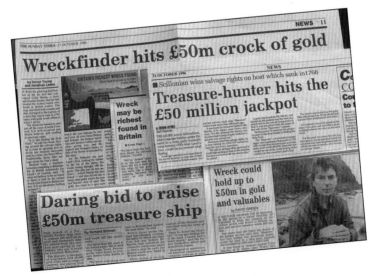

Since no gold was found – the projected £50 million was media speculation. RICHARD LARN COLLECTION

additional large sums of personal money and jewellery. Unfortunately, neither proved true, although artefact finds were spectacular. Excavation of the wreck revealed the unknown illegal cargo carried in her hold, namely 36 large iron cannon of differing calibres and gun-founders, plus boxes of flint-lock Tower muskets, iron shot of calibres different to the cannon carried by every Post Office packet. Captain Sherburn appears to have been engaged in gun-running or smuggling, bringing undeclared cannon and ammunition into the country, probably to sell to merchant ship owners. Unfortunately, the truth died with him, his motive presumably financial, we shall never know. The salvage operation ceased when English Heritage declared the site a Protected Wreck in 1998, being the only packet-ship wreck in UK waters. Despite court action, no further work on the wreck of the *Hanover* has been undertaken since. Twenty Finbanker cannon, part of the cargo, are currently being offered for sale at Kidderminster for £1,850 each.

The last but one sailing coaster, the Sarah Evans *was wrecked near Portreath on 27 October 1932. Built in 1877, she was 110-tons, and had an auxiliary petrol engine, which had failed.*

Le Landois

30 September 1837 – Sennen Cove, Land's End

Fog, common on the Cornish coast in both summer and winter, was responsible for one of the most notorious wrecking incidents in 1837. A Trinity House service yacht was engaged in the erection of a new beacon on the Wolf Rock that September. The sum of £11,298.4s 1d had been made available for a cast iron cone, 12ft in diameter and 22ft tall filled with masonry to be cemented to the rock base, which measures 525ft by 450ft and is always visible except at high spring tides. This in turn would hold a tall wooden mast topped with a 6ft diameter iron 'globe' painted red, but it took from 1836 to July 1840 to achieve, heavy seas making it impossible to land and continue work. Whilst anchored in Sennen Bay for shelter, the Trinity vessel was hailed by a large French brig named *Le Landois*; Captain Herbert, who asked for the best course to set for the Bristol Channel, and was told to steer north-west to clear the land, then north-east.

Dense fog then returned, the brig steered north-east by mistake, and drove ashore in a small cove called Boscriggan near Cape Cornwall. Her crew and passengers, numbering seventeen in total, managed to reach the shore, but with an onshore wind, the ship quickly went to pieces in heavy ground seas before dawn. Her cargo was extremely valuable and varied, so that cases of red and white wine in bottles, cordials, thousands of bundles of barrel staves, bales of cambric, velvet and cotton cloth and barrels of tobacco leaf lay heaped on the rocks or scattered across the beach. French brandy, rum and gin leaked out of damaged casks, filling rock pools, and the moment it became public knowledge, the locals descended on the area like locusts and proceeded to get drunk. Houses large and small emptied as farmers, labourers, fishermen, tin miners and their families fell on the shipwreck cargo – this was an opportunity not to be missed. The French Consul and Lloyd's Shipping Agent at Penzance, a Richard Pearce, whose responsibilities included protecting shipwrecks and their cargoes, found on arrival around noon that there were literally a thousand people engaged in plunder, many now drunk.

He did his best to organise a salvage party, but as fast as they saved cargo and piled it up above high tide, it disappeared! He sent to Penzance for the Revenue cutter *Sylvia* to get round to Land's End immediately, but on arrival they were insufficient in number to handle the situation. All day and night, the looting and drinking continued, and when Captain Sharp and 25 Coastguards eventually arrived on the scene, they faced an unruly, drunken mob now estimated at over 4,000. The 'wreckers' had pails and pots filled with wine or spirits, and as more men and women became paralytically drunk, neither side was prepared to give way. The Lloyd's Agent called on the Reverend Buller of St Just to read the Riot Act, which only incensed the mob further. A constable arrested a youth for stealing a bundle of staves, only to be attacked by the lad's father, and no sooner had the bundle been dropped than another 'wrecker' snatched it up and ran off. Both father and son refused to give their names, despite the agent offering anyone 20 guineas for the information, so both were jailed pending prosecution. A great deal of the cargo was blown or drifted north, so boatmen from Cape Cornwall to Pendeen participated in the windfall, and on such a remote and isolated coast the authorities were virtually helpless. It was said that for years the locals around St Just were still opening bottles from this wreck on special occasions, toasting their good fortune. As for the two men of St Just, whose surname was Ellis, the judiciary were determined to make an example of them when they appeared before Judge Scobell at the quarter sessions at Bodmin on 17th October, charged with having feloniously stolen a quantity of staves, being the merchandise of a ship. Witnesses swore that neither men were anywhere near the wreck, but the evidence given by the Lloyd's Agent led to the son being found guilty and sentenced to be hanged. Fortunately, this was later commuted to transportation to Australia for life, which was rough justice, considering the numbers of people present at the wreck, and that this was the only prosecution.

She was launched as HM Monitor M-22 for the Royal Navy. Following WW1 her gun was removed and she was converted to a mine-layer and given the name HMS Medea. On her way to the breakers yard in Wales, she broke adrift from a tug off Padstow, going ashore on Greenaway rocks on 28 January 1939.

RICHARD LARN COLLECTION

New Commercial

11 January 1851 – the Brisons, Land's End

The stationing of the first lifeboat at Sennen Cove, Land's End, came about following the wreck of this 250-ton *Whitby* registered snow – a type of brig – the *New Commercial*. She was outward bound from the River Mersey to Jamaica with a general cargo. After leaving the Irish Sea, she encountered a severe south-westerly gale accompanied by fog which forced her dangerously close inshore to Cape Cornwall. She had barely cleared the coast when out of the murk loomed what appeared to be two ships close together, which proved not to be ships at all but the Brisons, two very large rocks close together, three miles north of Land's End.

Built at Sunderland in 1847, she was carrying a crew of nine, plus Captain Sanderson's wife, when she drove ashore on a ledge of rock between the Great and Little Brison, immediately going to pieces. All on board found shelter on a precarious ledge on the Little Brison, but around 9am on the flood tide, they were washed into the sea by a huge wave. Only a mulatto seaman named Isaac Williams, the captain and his wife could swim; they managed to remain afloat whilst the rest of the crew drowned. The seaman found a piece of wreck timber large enough on which he could sit, and aided by a small plank as an improvised paddle and a scrap of canvas as a make-shift sail, got clear of the rocks to be rescued by Sennen fishermen. Meanwhile the captain's wife, assisted by her husband, had scrambled back onto the rock finding shelter above the elements in a small cleft.

Fortunately, for them, a vigilant Cape Cornwall coastguard witnessed their plight at day break, and sent to St Ives for the Revenue cutter *Sylvia* to assist, at the same time alerting the villagers in Sennen of the wreck. By now, the cliffs overlooking the site, less than a mile away were, if we can believe newspaper reports of the time, crowded with over 2,000 spectators. As soon as the *Sylvia* arrived her crew launched a boat, and manned by four seamen under Commander Forward, they attempted a rescue but were unable to get close to the Brisons due to heavy seas.

As darkness fell and still unable to effect a rescue, the cutter stood off, leaving the two survivors on the rock in heavy rain and wind that lasted all night. Next day was a Sunday, and from dawn the cliffs were swarming with people, who witnessed no less than three fishing boats, another craft manned by coastguards and a Revenue boat from Pendeen, all converge on the Brisons intent on rescue. By now, spectators were said to number between five and six thousand, who cheered each boat as it came into view. The Pendeen boat brought out a Dennett life-saving nine pounder rocket apparatus, which had never before been used by the local coastguard. At some risk to himself in such a confined space, since the instructions recommended operators should be several feet to the rear of rockets before firing, Captain Davies fired a line which fell across the rocks but then parted on a sharp ledge. However, a second was successfully held by Captain Sanderson who tied the line around his wife's waist. He was seen encouraging her to jump into the sea, but it was some long time before the petrified woman could pluck up sufficient courage to do so. Bare foot and wearing only a thin woollen nightdress, she was dragged through the waves to the boat, then lifted inboard. Exhausted, very cold and suffering extreme hypothermia, she died before the boat reached Sennen Cove.

The captain tied another rocket line round his own waist, leapt into the sea and was saved in the same manner, the poor man learning of his wife's demise only when he stepped ashore at the cove. The National Shipwreck Institution for the Preservation of Life from Shipwreck, as the RNLI was then known, awarded a gold medal to Commander Forward of the Sylvia, with silver medals to his six boat crew, also a gold to Captain Davies and his four boatmen, plus a further 11 silver to local Sennen boatmen. In June 1853 the Institution created the first lifeboat station at Sennen Cove, which is open to this day and extremely active.

The ss Umbré *was carrying a general cargo from Liverpool when she met with fog off Cornwall, and on 20 February 1899 she ran into Morvah Cliffs, near Pendeen.* ST IVES STUDIO

SS *Nile*

30 November 1854 – The Stones, near St Ives

So many ships had been lost on the Stones reef off St Ives, that Trinity House were considering the erection of a lighthouse on Godrevy Island, when the tragic loss of the *Nile* in November 1854 brought the matter to a head. There is no exact count of the number of ships wrecked on the Outer and Inner Stones or Godrevy Island, but eighteen names are recorded.

Owned by the British & Irish Steam Packet Co Ltd, the ss *Nile* was on passage from Liverpool to Penzance when she was lost at night, in the pitch dark and a howling gale, on 30 November 1854. Built at Greenock just five years earlier, she was 700 tons, screw propulsion, with a 2-cylinder compound engine and one boiler, carrying a crew of sixteen and twenty-four passengers under Captain Moppett. Stylish for her day, she carried three raked masts and sails, a tall spindly funnel, bowsprit and figurehead, and gave every appearance of speed and efficiency. She plied regularly between Liverpool, Plymouth and London, calling at intermediary ports as weather and circumstances permitted.

Unfortunately, she was beginning to earn a reputation as an unlucky ship, since in July 1854 a Cornish mining passenger named Matthew Heath, fell through the engine-room skylight and was killed. Then she was in collision off Plymouth's breakwater where she ran down and sank the Looe smack, *William & Anne*, causing the death of her captain.

She sailed prematurely from Liverpool on 28 November 1854, ignoring her printed timetable and schedule, leaving several passengers behind. A Captain Perry and his family arrived to find her berth empty. A Cornishman from Newlyn put his bags onboard then went for a walk ashore, missing her departure. She also left without her Irish Channel pilot, who arrived on the dockside to find her gangway already pulled up and her captain unwilling to lower it again. Several Cornish people were on board, Edward Trewavas, son of a Mousehole fisherman, another Mousehole man, Captain Frederick Gruzelier, bringing home from Belfast his bride of four weeks; a John Treweek and a John Ivens of Penzance. There were also five other passengers, including Mrs Hallaghan of Falmouth, and her child. Her holds full of Manchester goods destined for shops in Cornwall and Plymouth, she was already hours behind schedule due to heavy gales when she called at Bristol. Only one ship sighted the *Nile* after Bristol, the Cork packet *Sylph* in the evening of 30th November, off Lundy, evidently southbound for Land's End.

What happened thereafter is speculation, since no one survived the wreck, but something presumably went wrong, possibly engine failure, steering trouble, a serious compass error – we shall never know. Between 2 and 3 am she struck the Outer Stones and sank, none of her boats getting away. Next day the area was strewn with shipwreck cargo, porter barrels, casks, crates, boxes, bolts of cloth, books, paper, bunks and even a writing desk. Among the first recoveries on Portreath beach was a tied handkerchief containing a bible, prayer book and ship's discharge certificate of Edward Trewavas. Only one body was found, that of 60-year old Hannah Lamb, 'spinster', of Devonport, found under Camborne Cliff and buried in Illogan church. The topmasts of the wreck showed above the surface a mile to the north of the Stones, until a gale caused the wreck to break up, spewing out huge quantities of butter, lard, beef, oatmeal and tallow, which came ashore on Hayle Bar.

The steam packet Nile *which struck the Stones Reef off St Ives in 1854.*
PAINTING BY THE LATE CLIVE CARTER

Bencoolen

Bencoolen

21 October 1862 – Budehaven

A privately owned East Indiaman, the Honourable English East India Company having gone into liquidation in 1834, the *Bencoolen* a barque of 1,415 tons, which had been built in New Brunswick in 1855, was intended to travel half way round the world when wrecked near Bude. She sailed from Liverpool bound for Bombay on 13 October, carrying a general cargo, which included a large quantity of iron, having on board 31 crew under Captain Chambers.

Shortly after rounding Anglesey and entering the Irish Sea, she ran into a SW gale and began to make 11 inches of water an hour (the ship sinking by this amount, but the captain refused to turn back. Three days later her mainsail was blown away, and not long after, when 40 miles west of the Tuskar Rock, her foretop mast collapsed. This was followed by the foremast itself, which in falling caused both her main and mizzen masts to break off at deck level despite being made of iron. Two seamen, who were in the rigging at the time, fell into the sea and drowned. By now, the ship was in serious distress, the leak having increased and all her boats being smashed to pieces as the masts fell on top of them.

Driven before the wind into the Bristol Channel, the crew were employed in making a raft of spare spars and booms, in case they sank. When land was sighted ahead to starboard, a jury-rig boom and sail was erected and they steered for the shore, the ship grounding to the eastward of the entrance to Bude Haven. Meanwhile Captain Chambers had gone to his cabin where he proceeded to get drunk. He returned to the poop deck but fell down several times, then returned to his cabin, got into his bunk and was never seen again. Two of the crew went below at different times as the ship neared the shore, asking him to come on deck and get on the raft, but he refused to leave his cabin and drowned as the ship broke up.

Bude coastguards set up their rocket apparatus and attempted to get a line to the ship. The first rocket hit the side of the vessel and fell into the sea; the ship's second Mate got hold of the second but was pulled overboard and drowned. A third line fell clean across the wreck but before anyone could grasp it, a tremendous wave broke over the ship and she commenced to break up. Only minutes later the entire forecastle was carried away, taking with it the raft so carefully put together by the men who now clung to it in the hope of salvation. When it eventually hit the rocks its occupants were catapulted into the surf zone, only boatswain Thomas Aspinwall, and seamen Andrew Hallman, John Whiteside, George Walsh and two others surviving. The bodies of the Chief Mate and thirteen seamen were eventually recovered and laid to rest in a mass grave in Bude churchyard. The loss of the vessel was attributed to her standing rigging which was made of wire being slack from the moment she sailed, not having been set up correctly, despite having been overhauled by dockyard workers whilst in Liverpool.

ss *Malta*

15 October 1889 - Cape Cornwall

Residents of West Penwith were still talking about the wreck of the steamship *Asia* on 31 August 1889 on the Bridges Rocks, near Cape Cornwall, and the fact that the 57-ton smack *Elizabeth* had run into the wreck the very next day when, 45 days later, there was a new wreck in the area. This was the Cunard Line's ss *Malta*, 2,244 tons gross, carrying a general cargo from Liverpool to Genoa. No one was aware she had driven ashore half a mile east of Cape Cornwall until she was spotted by tin miners going to work at the nearby cliff-top Botallack mine. Already 24 years old the *Malta* was almost at the end of a particular shipbuilding era, so that whilst being a steamship, she carried two masts with sails, a long bowsprit and a female bust figurehead.

Carrying a crew of 40 and 21 passengers, she was close to Land's End when she ran into thick fog, but Captain Lavis decided not to reduce speed since the elderly ship could barely make nine knots against a head tide anyway. A member of the crew had just been instructed to commence taking soundings with a lead and line, when the lookout sighted breakers dead ahead, and the ship slid gracefully ashore under the headland cliffs of Kenidjack Castle. Initially, no one on board realised they were in fact shipwrecked; since all was quiet except for what they thought was the ship's engine, but was in fact the iron stamps crushing tin ore at the nearby mine workings!

A lifeboat was launched carrying all the passengers, who landed safely. The ship had only flooded in the forward part so the crew remained aboard, hoping that Falmouth tugs would refloat her, but on their arrival despite every effort, the *Malta* refused to move. By 11am, a heavy ground sea set in and the ship commenced to pound heavily on the rocks, and after baggage, stores and deck gear was taken off, she was abandoned.

Within 24-hours, the wind increased to gale force from the WNW, and by dawn her funnel and masts had collapsed and the hull broken in two. Her cargo commenced to come ashore, and the locals could hardly believe their eyes. Bolts of velveteen, calico, muslin, linen bed sheets, rugs and carpets, casks of palm oil, kegs of spirits, handkerchiefs, bottles of beer and wine and rolls of india-rubber littered the shore. At the Board of Trade inquiry, her captain was found guilty of failing to navigate with due care and attention, and his certificate as a ship's master was withdrawn for 3 months.

The Malta *went shore in fog under Castle Kenidjack on 15 October 1889. Her forty crew and twenty one passengers were all saved, but they lost all their baggage and valuables when the boat carrying them capsized.*

ss *Escurial*

25 January 1895 – Portreath

A minor collision between this 1,158-tons gross iron steamship and a small 40-ton wooden Welsh pilot cutter at sea was, at the time, considered a minor and insignificant accident, since neither vessel appeared to have been damaged, but in fact, it brought about the loss of the *Escurial*. The Glasgow registered steamship, built in 1879 by Alexander Stephens of Govan, had loaded 1,350 tons of coal at Cardiff and was outward bound for the Adriatic port of Fiume. By noon on 24 January 1895, when ploughing though heavy seas with an overcast sky threatening snow, Captain Andrews noticed that his ship had assumed a slight list to starboard, and ordered the 2nd Officer to summon the ship's carpenter to sound the bilges. His report came back that there was a severe leak somewhere forward of the engine-room, caused by the collision, but that so far the donkey engine bilge pump was able to contain the inflow.

The list slowly got worse and soon the water level was increasing as the pump became choked with coal dust and debris. Heavy seas were now breaking across the deck, one smashing the glass in an engine-room skylight, allowing seawater to soak into a drive belt, which in turn drove a boiler forced draught fan. The sodden belt commenced to slip, the fan ceased to turn and as the boiler temperature dropped so did the steam pressure and consequently the ship's speed. Worse was to follow as the sea tore open the tarpaulin covering the after hatch, then smashed some wooden hatch covers, allowing more water into the ship. An hour later, with the boiler-room plates lifting under pressure of bilge water, her fires were extinguished, and the ship's officers were forced to consider their options.

The entire crew of nineteen were mustered on deck, lifejackets were handed out and distress rockets fired, whilst with the captain's permission the steward served out a tot of rum to each man. At that moment the 3rd Engineer, David Martin of Dundee, saw the flash of a lighthouse which was recognised as that on Godrevy Island, not far from St Ives. At 7.30am the port anchor was dropped close to a set of rocks with the unusual name of 'Man and his Man' (see the story of the *Hanover*), but with the ship sinking ever deeper and her anchor dragging across the seabed she ended up under Gull Rock, hard aground on a shallow sandy bottom. The coastguards fired rocket after rocket in an attempt to rig a breeches buoy, but with the ship so far out they all fell short. Some of the crew jumped overboard, determined to save themselves by swimming ashore through the breakers.

Meanwhile onshore the Hayle lifeboat *E F Harrison* which had been brought to Portreath by road became stuck in soft sand on the beach, and it was some time before it could be launched. One of the crew who swam ashore, fireman James Nolan, then appeared alongside the lifeboat, but in the short time it took to pull him to safety, the lifeboat drifted beam on to the beach back where she had started from. It was now impossible to re-launch. Any hope of rescue from ashore disappeared when the St Ives' lifeboat turned back off Godrevy due to a signalling error by the lighthouse keepers; the boat from Newquay was almost wrecked whilst trying to get it off its carriage, and a Padstow – based tug would not arrive for at least another six hours.

On board the ship it was now a case of every man for himself, the crew either throwing themselves into the sea or were picked up off the deck by huge waves. On Portreath beach, the scene was unforgettable as coastguards, fishermen, lifeboat men, all wearing lifejackets plunged into the surf time after time to drag part drowned seamen ashore. The sea turned black as the coal cargo washed out of the wreck, the collapse of her foremast throwing a solitary seaman into the sea, five others joining him when the mainmast fell. It then began to snow very heavily blotting out the wreck from ashore. A muster of the survivors showed that eleven men were unaccounted for, and as the night wore on, it was obvious these had drowned, although a search was resumed at daybreak, which reported only corpses being washed ashore along with wreckage.

The Hayle lifeboat prepares to launch to go to the assistance of the ss Escurial 25 January 1895. RICHARD LARN COLLECTION

Full-rigged ship
Alexander Yeats

25 September 1896 – Gurnard's Head, near St Ives

Today, when a ship sets off from one port to another, invariably it will take the shortest route, and accidents excepting, would expect to arrive safely in the shortest possible time, but there have been many occasions when quite the opposite happened. The story of the *Alexander Yeats* is one such incident, when her voyage went unbelievably wrong, due entirely to weather.

A large three-masted wooden vessel of 1,589-tons gross, she had been built at Portland, New Brunswick in 1876 for Alexander Yeats & Sons, which explains how she acquired her name. Registered at St John, she was later sold to George Windron of Liverpool, and her last voyage was intended to be from Darien, in Georgia, to Devonport Dockyard via Holyhead to deliver a cargo of pitch-pine logs. She reached Holyhead, sailing from there under tow of the tug *Gamecock* on 19 September 1896 and all went well until both vessels were off the South Bishops, west of Milford Haven. Bad weather caused them to reverse course in an attempt to return to Holyhead, but then the towing cable parted and unable to reconnect it, the *Alexander Yeats* set her sails in an attempt to find a sheltered haven. She no sooner had some canvas up than it was blown to shreds, and even heavier storm canvas went the same way. Now dangerously close to Milford, within

The Alexander Yeats hard and fast as indicated by her waterline, her deck cargo having been thrown overboard.

a day she was off Portreath. By 24 September, she found herself close to the Wolf Rock, then the wind shifted and she was back off St Agnes, totally out of control.

By now the ship was unmanageable on account of her heavy deck load of timber, and Captain Browning and his 1st Mate, Robert Jones, both from Liverpool, agreed that their best course of action would be to run the ship ashore, but dare not tell the crew. Unbeknown to the ship, coastguards at Portreath had spotted their plight and called out the Hayle lifeboat, but heavy seas prevented it crossing Hayle Bar and it returned to its station. The ship became embayed off Gurnard's Head, to the NW of St Ives, and was run ashore in a small cove. The St Ives Rocket Brigade made contact, setting up a breeches buoy by means of which the ship's polyglot crew of 19 were safely landed. During the salvage of her cargo, rafts of up to 100 logs were lashed together, then towed by the Hayle tug *North Star* round to St Ives harbour and beached. On 28 September the Salvage Association declared the vessel had hogged*, the tide was now flowing freely through the ship and she was a total loss. The *Alexander Yeats* then commenced to break up, her stern, complete with name, drifting as far as Portreath beach before going ashore. On 12 October the wreck went completely to pieces, the timber within her hold littering the coast for miles, a useful and welcome bounty to the residents of Penwith.

Footnote – *hogged – that is whilst her midships section was supported, her bow and stern were not so that the waves caused her to see-saw and break her back.*

Full-rigged ship
Seine

28 December 1900 – Perranporth

The breeches buoy apparatus that saved so many lives from shipwreck was put to the test when this French nitrate clipper stranded on the 28th December. Eighty-one days out from Iquiquie carrying 2,500 tons of saltpetre bound to Falmouth 'for orders', she ran into a WNW gale off the Isles of Scilly at which point Captain Quimper gave up any idea of being able to reach Falmouth in the storm. The ship headed off up the north coast of Cornwall, reaching St Agnes before they found any degree of shelter. At 10am the local coastguards saw her in difficulty offshore with most of her sails blown away, damage to her rigging and even her reefed topsails streaming out in ribbons from her yards.

The Perranporth and St Agnes rocket brigade were called out and assembled in anticipation which was timely, since in attempting a course change by tacking, the *Seine* grounded on a sandy beach off Perran, just north of Chapel Rock. Nine life-saving rockets were fired at the ship against the strong wind but all missed, falling into the sea. The 10th rocket finally took a line clean between her masts, but there was a delay whilst the rocket crew spliced two hawsers together to make one long enough, since the vessel was so far out. A breeches buoy was eventually set up and six sailors and a delirious cabin boy, out of her crew of 24, landed safely. Then the ship rolled violently in a swell and the hawser parted rendering the rescue apparatus useless. At this point as the tide dropped, six Newquay men waded out towards the wreck catching a line thrown from the bow enabling five crew to slide down into five feet of water, Captain Quimper being the last to leave.

By morning, the barque was on her beam-ends, dismasted, gutted and open to the elements, breaking up on the following high tide. Her cargo washed out, so that the Cornish 'wreckers' were disappointed, there being very little left to salvage.

The Seine *was wrecked near Droskyn Head, on Perranporth beach at 11am on 28 December 1900. The wreck was sold for £42, but quickly became engulfed in the sand; occasionally parts of the wreck are exposed as the sand shifts.* GIBSONS OF SCILLY

ss *Bessemer City*

1 November 1936 – Brea Cove, near St.Ives

O f all the shipwrecks that have occurred in the St
Ives area, it was the steamship *Bessemer City* that
left the greatest impression on the local
population. This was due not to loss of life, since her captain
and all 33 crew on board were saved, nor due to any dramatic
cliff-top rescue by breeches-buoy, since the St Ives lifeboat
saved the entire crew, but to the nature of her cargo.
Smuggling had long ceased by 1939, but the sheer volume,
variety and illegal benefit her cargo brought to the population
of the area far outweighed anything the locals had ever seen
or heard of by way of shipwreck bounty, either before or since.

Built by the Chickasaw Shipbuilding Corporation at
Chicksaw, USA. in 1920, owned by the Isthmian SS Co and
registered at New York, the *Bessemer City* was a large ship of
5,686-gross tons, and her four boilers fed two steam turbine
engines. She was on passage from New Westminster in
California to London via Liverpool when, on 1 November
1936, she drove ashore in Brea Cove in dense fog at 9.45pm,
three miles west of St Ives. How she managed to be so far off-
course is still something of a mystery, since she should have
been rounding Land's End at the time. Instead she was closer
to Godrevy Island and well off course, fog the only possible
explanation. Land's End Radio picked up her distress call,
which advised she was ashore, leaking badly; and in need of
assistance. Unknown to Captain Joseph Herman, it was a John
Eddy of Trevalgan Farm who first alerted the authorities,

Of 5,686 tons gross, built in 1921 at Alabama, USA, powered by two steam turbines geared to a single shaft this steel steamship left Liverpool for London on 31 October 1936 to complete discharging her general cargo of foodstuffs from America. In reduced visibility she drove ashore the following day under Trevalgan Cliff, near Clodgy Point, St Ives.

STUDIO ST IVES

having heard the loud grating sound of the ship going ashore, which completely 'spooked' his cattle, causing them to panic and run around their field. Looking down from Pen Enys Point, having seen deck lights and the outline of a ship, he telephoned the Coastguard. The maroons went off at midnight and the St Ives lifeboat *Caroline Parsons* was afloat and making for the wreck in 15 minutes. It took three trips to save all her crew and later a fourth to return Captain Herman to his ship.

She broke in two whilst the crew were still being rescued, and by daybreak on 2 October was in two halves, at right angles to each other and over 100ft (30m) apart, which says a great deal for the power of the sea, especially since conditions were not that rough. The Salvage Association inspected the wreck from the top of the sheer cliffs, reporting that she was unapproachable from the weather side and was definitely a total loss. Then the owners set about arranging with the Penzance based Western Marine Salvage Company, the recovery of as much cargo, stores and equipment as possible.

So what was special about her cargo? On deck, she carried a part load of lumber, 500 tons of cut softwood planks for the building industry, and in her lower holds, over 200 tons of refined zinc in ingot form. Between decks were an incredible 70,000 cases of food. This comprised every sort of Californian tinned and dried fruit. Peaches, apricots, pineapple, pears, plums, apples and oranges, as well as raisins and sultanas, tinned salmon, beef and meats and countless other delicacies, the like of which some in Cornwall had never seen, let alone tasted. Little was salvaged officially, the bulk finding its way into kitchen cupboards and attics the length of Penwith, or else outhouses for a 'rainy-day'. It proved something of a lottery, since all the labels came off once wet and few knew what the contents of a tin were likely to be until opened. It is said that in St Ives, tins from this wreck supplemented many a meal during the austere food rationing years of WW2 yet to come.

mv *Mulheim*

22 March 2003 – Gamper Bay, Land's End

Myriad different circumstances have caused ships to be wrecked, but the most bizarre must surely be the incident that brought about the wreck of this 1,846-tonne coaster the *Mulheim*. She was carrying 2,300 tonnes of shredded plastic from scrap motor vehicles, on passage from Cork to Lubec, her crew asleep in their bunks with the 1st mate on the bridge seated in the watch chair. As the ship made its way down the Irish Sea intent on rounding Land's End, the officer-of-the-watch went to stand up, caught a pocket of his trousers on the chair's footplate lever, fell over and knocked himself unconscious!

How long he remained in this state is uncertain, but by the time he recovered and picked himself up off the deck, the ship was close inshore and heading for the cliffs, where she ran aground. The incident had similarities to the loss of the container feeder ship mv *Cita* in the Isles of Scilly, six years previously, when the watch-officer admitted falling asleep!

As she went ashore rocks tore huge holes in her hull and some 75-tonnes of diesel fuel spilled into the sea, making recovery of the vessel impossible. The emphasis then shifted to controlling a potential spill of the plastic chippings she carried, in addition to a quantity of lead acid batteries and containers of paint. The ship lay in an extremely exposed position under 20m high cliffs in Gamper Bay, close to the

Sennen Cove lifeboat station, leaving her at the mercy of any westerly wind. Speedy action was of the essence if a major environmental disaster was to be averted. A quarter of her cargo, some 4-500 tonnes of pvc had already escaped, resulting in a bank of floating debris 50m long, much of which went ashore on Sennen beach. Headed by the Maritime Salvage & Intervention Group, Maritime Coastguard Agency and Cornwall's County Council, a salvage unit was set up to co-ordinate the work. A mini jack-up rig with a crane was placed alongside the wreck on 10 April, which using a grab dropped the cargo into a barge. Then a change for the worse in the weather dictated that the rig and barge had to be moved to safety, having worked for only six days.

Access between the wreck and the cliff top was then achieved by means of a rope walkway, allowing a conveyor belt to be set up, the pvc now being taken ashore and loaded into lorries. By 11 May following a severe battering in a gale, the *Mulheim* showed signs of breaking up, and on 30 May salvage recovery concluded leaving less than ten tonnes in her hold. By now she was a major tourist attraction, with thousands of sightseers visiting daily. So many people wanted to see the wreck, fields became temporary car parks, and local shops and cafes admitted they had never had a season like it. On 31 October that year, the sea threw the main part of the wreck into Castle Zawn cove, and over the winter, it went to pieces. Her rusting stern section still shows at low tide, five years after the event, the last major wreck in Cornwall to date.